States

WISCONSIN

by Bridget Parker

CAPSTONE PRESS
a capstone imprint

Next Page Books are published by Capstone Press,
1710 Roe Crest Drive, North Mankato, Minnesota 56003
www.mycapstone.com

Library of Congress Cataloging-in-Publication Data
Cataloging-in-publication information is on file with the Library of
Congress.
ISBN 978-1-5157-0438-6 (library binding)
ISBN 978-1-5157-0497-3 (paperback)
ISBN 978-1-5157-0549-9 (ebook PDF)

Editorial Credits
Jaclyn Jaycox, editor; Kazuko Collins and Katy LaVigne, designers;
Morgan Walters, media researcher; Tori Abraham, production specialist

Photo Credits
Alamy: ZUMA Press, Inc., 10; Capstone Press: Angi Gahler, map 4,
7; CriaImages.com: Jay Robert Nash Collection, top 18, middle 18;
Dreamstime: J.Schelkle, bottom left 21, Louis Horch, 29, Radomír
Režný, middle right 21, Suzanne Tucker, 16; Getty Images: Fototeca
Storica Nazionale, 26, ullstein bild, 12; Library of Congress Rare Book
and Special Collections Division Washington, D.C., top 19; iStockphoto:
ZU_09, 27; Newscom: Dennis Brack b37, bottom 18, STACEY WESCOTT/
KRT, 11, 28; North Wind Picture Archives, 25; One Mile Up, Inc.,
flag, seal 23; Shutterstock: BKingFoto, 6, Chris Hill, bottom left 20,
Christopher Halloran, middle 19, Cristina Negoita, top right 21,
Critterbiz, bottom right 8, Daniel Prudek, bottom right 21, Everett
Collection, bottom 19, Gerald A. DeBoer, bottom left 8, James Ward
Ewing, 7, Jenoche, top 24, Kletr, bottom right 20, Kunal Mehta, 9,
Laura Mountainspring, top left 21, MaraZe, 15, Mark Herreid, bottom
24, Nancy Gill, cover, oksana2010, top right 20, outdoorsman, middle
left 21, pyzata, 14, Rudy Balasko, 5, TouchingPixel, 13, youngryand,
17, Zamada, top left 20

All design elements by Shutterstock

Printed and bound in China.
0316/CA21600187
012016   009436F16

TABLE OF CONTENTS

Want to take your research further? Ask your librarian if your school subscribes to PebbleGo Next. If so, when you see this helpful symbol (↖) throughout the book, log onto www.pebblegonext.com for bonus downloads and information.

Wisconsin is shaped like a big mitten. The "thumb" is the Door Peninsula. It sticks out into Lake Michigan. Lake Michigan also forms Wisconsin's eastern border. Illinois lies south of Wisconsin. Minnesota and Iowa lie to the west, across the Mississippi and Saint Croix rivers. On the north is Lake Superior. Michigan's Upper Peninsula meets northeast Wisconsin. Madison, the state capital, is in south-central Wisconsin. Wisconsin's biggest cities are Madison, Milwaukee, Green Bay, Kenosha, and Racine.

PebbleGo Next Bonus!
To print and label your own map, go to **www.pebblegonext.com** and search keywords:

WI MAP

Milwaukee lies on the western shores of Lake Michigan. Its name comes from the American Indian word "Milliocki," which means "gathering place by the water."

GEOGRAPHY

Wisconsin has five land regions. They are the Northern Highland, the Central Plain, the Lake Superior Lowland, the Eastern Ridges and Lowlands, and the Western Upland. The Northern Highland is in north-central Wisconsin. Wisconsin's highest point is found here. Timms Hill rises 1,952 feet (595 meters) above sea level. Swamps, wetlands, and rivers cover the Central Plain. The Lake Superior Lowland is in northern Wisconsin. It is a small plain about 20 miles (32 kilometers) wide. The Eastern Ridges and Lowlands region in southeastern Wisconsin has rolling hills and rich soil. The hilly Western Upland follows the Mississippi River to the border of Illinois.

PebbleGo Next Bonus! To watch a video about the Apostle Islands, go to www.pebblegonext.com and search keywords:

WI VIDEO

Glaciers passed through Wisconsin thousands of years ago, which aided in the formation of the state's five land regions.

The Bababoo Hills are made up of ocean sediment that was deposited billions of years ago.

Apostle Islands

Lake Superior

LAKE SUPERIOR LOWLAND

Montreal River

St. Croix River

NORTHERN HIGHLAND

Menominee River

▲ Timms Hill

CENTRAL PLAIN

Chippewa River

CENTRAL PLAIN

Green Bay

WESTERN UPLAND

Mississippi River

Fox River

Green Lake

Lake Winnebago

Wisconsin River

EASTERN RIDGES AND LOWLANDS

Lake Michigan

Legend

▲ Highest Point

⬭ Lake

〜 River

Scale

Miles
0   20   40   60   80

0 20 40 60 80 100
Kilometers

7

WEATHER

Wisconsin's summers are warm. Winters are long and cold. Wisconsin's average summer temperature is 67 degrees Fahrenheit (19 degrees Celsius). The average winter temperature is 18°F (-8°C).

Average High and Low Temperatures (Milwaukee, WI)

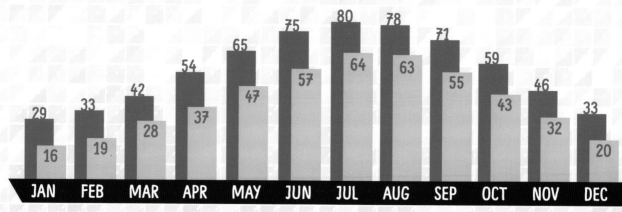

	JAN	FEB	MAR	APR	MAY	JUN	JUL	AUG	SEP	OCT	NOV	DEC
High	29	33	42	54	65	75	80	78	71	59	46	33
Low	16	19	28	37	47	57	64	63	55	43	32	20

LANDMARKS

Door County

Door County is a popular vacation spot on the Door Peninsula in eastern Wisconsin. Door County has 300 miles (483 km) of scenic shoreline, five state parks, and 11 historic lighthouses. Tourists enjoy Door County's famous fish boils and beautiful countryside.

House on the Rock

In Spring Green in southwestern Wisconsin, visitors can see the amazing House on the Rock. This large house is perched on top of a rock. Its Infinity Room extends far over the valley. The house is full of many collections, including dollhouses and tiny circuses. It also has one of the world's largest carousels, with 269 handcrafted animals and 20,000 lights.

Wisconsin Dells

Wisconsin Dells in southern Wisconsin is home to one of the country's largest indoor water parks. Waterslides, air tubes, and millions of gallons of water bring families from around the country to Wisconsin Dells every summer. Visitors to the Dells enjoy many outdoor activities. People hike, explore caves, and go horseback riding.

HISTORY AND GOVERNMENT

Jean Nicolet arrived on the Wisconsin shore of Lake Michigan in 1634.

American Indians had been living in Wisconsin for thousands of years before Europeans arrived. In 1634 French explorer Jean Nicolet canoed across Lake Michigan from Canada. In 1673 French explorers Jacques Marquette and Louis Jolliet sailed down the Fox River into the middle of Wisconsin. In 1763 the British gained control of the Wisconsin area. American colonists gained their freedom from Great Britain after winning the Revolutionary War (1775–1783). In 1783 the United States gained control of the Wisconsin area. The U.S. government set up the Wisconsin Territory in 1836. Wisconsin became the 30th state in 1848.

Wisconsin's state government has three branches. The governor leads the executive branch, which carries out laws. The legislature is made up of the 33-member Senate and the 99-member Assembly. Judges and their courts make up the judicial branch. They uphold the laws.

Wisconsin's state capitol building was named a National Historic Landmark in 2001.

INDUSTRY

Wisconsin has a diverse economy. Its people work in a variety of jobs and businesses. Agriculture, manufacturing, and service industries are the largest.

Wisconsin is one of the nation's leading agricultural states. It is often called America's Dairyland. Wisconsin's cheese factories make about 25 percent of the country's cheese. Milk and eggs are also important farm products. Wisconsin's other leading crops include corn, hay, soybeans, potatoes, snap beans, and oats.

Cows are raised for dairy as one of the state's major farming industries.

Most of the state's manufacturing plants are located in Milwaukee. Wisconsin's main manufactured products include food products, paper, automobiles, machinery, and chemicals.

Most of the state's workers have jobs in service industries, such as banking, education, health care, and tourism. People come to Wisconsin to hunt, hike, camp, swim, fish, and boat.

Cheesemakers in Wisconsin produce more than 600 varieties of cheese.

POPULATION

More than 83 percent of people in Wisconsin have European backgrounds. Many European immigrants came to the state during the 1800s and 1900s. More than half of Wisconsin residents have German backgrounds. Many others are from Ireland, Poland, Norway, and England. African-Americans make up about 6 percent of the state's population. Most of Wisconsin's African-Americans live in Milwaukee. Hispanics make up about 6 percent of the state's population. About 2 percent of Wisconsin's residents are Asian. American Indians make up about 1 percent of the state's population. They include Oneida, Ojibwa, Ho-Chunk, Stockbridge-Munsee, Menominee, and Brothertown Indians.

Population by Ethnicity

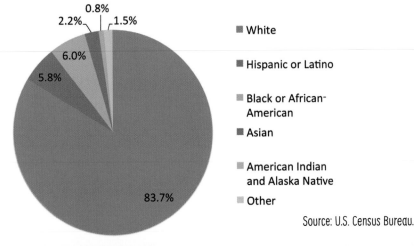

- 0.8%
- 2.2%
- 1.5%
- 6.0%
- 5.8%
- 83.7%

- White
- Hispanic or Latino
- Black or African-American
- Asian
- American Indian and Alaska Native
- Other

Source: U.S. Census Bureau.

FAMOUS PEOPLE

Frank Lloyd Wright (1867–1959) was an architect. He designed many famous buildings in his Prairie style, which blended with nature. He was born in Richland Center.

Orson Welles (1915–1985) was an actor and movie director. *Citizen Kane* (1941) is his most famous movie. He was born in Kenosha.

Georgia O'Keeffe (1887–1986) was an artist who painted huge, colorful flowers and other objects. She was born in Sun Prairie.

Harry Houdini (1874–1926) was a magician who was famous for his amazing escape acts. He escaped from locked crates, straightjackets, handcuffs, and prison cells. He was born in Budapest, Hungary. His family moved to Appleton when he was young.

Paul Ryan (1970–) is a politican. Since 1999 he has represented Wisconsin in the U.S. House of Representatives. He was the Republican Party nominee for vice president in the 2012 presidential election. In 2015 he was elected as the Speaker for the U.S. House of Representatives. He was born in Janesville.

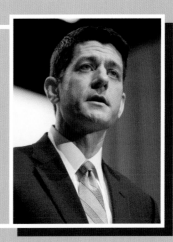

Danica Patrick (1982–) is a race car driver. In 2005 she placed fourth in the Indianapolis 500. She became the first woman to win an IndyCar race in 2008. In 2013 she won the time trials at the Daytona 500. She was born in Beloit.

STATE SYMBOLS

Tree

sugar maple

Flower

wood violet

Bird

robin

Fish

muskellunge

PebbleGo Next Bonus! To make a dessert using Wisconsin's leading fruit, go to www.pebblegonext.com and search keywords:

WI RECIPE

Peace Symbol

mourning dove

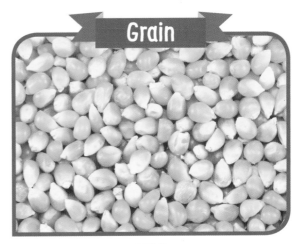

Grain

corn

Animal

badger

Dog

American water spaniel

Rock

red granite

Insect

honeybee

21

FAST FACTS

STATEHOOD
1848

CAPITAL ☆
Madison

LARGEST CITY •
Milwaukee

SIZE
54,158 square miles (140,269 square kilometers) land area (2010 U.S. Census Bureau)

POPULATION
5,742,713 (2013 U.S. Census estimate)

STATE NICKNAME
Badger State

STATE MOTTO
"Forward"

PebbleGo Next Bonus!
To learn the lyrics to the state song, go to www.pebblegonext.com and search keywords:

WI SONG

STATE SEAL

Wisconsin's state seal includes the state's coat of arms. The state's motto, "Forward," appears at the top of the seal. Several pictures on the seal represent important features in Wisconsin. The badger is the state animal. A sailor stands for people who work on Wisconsin's rivers and lakes. A miner stands for the state's mining business. Lead bars and a horn filled with fruit are symbols of Wisconsin's natural resources. The shield also has images that stand for manufacturing, agriculture, and shipping.

PebbleGo Next Bonus! To print and color your own flag, go to www.pebblegonext.com and search keywords: **WI FLAG**

STATE FLAG

Wisconsin adopted its official state flag in 1913. The flag is dark blue with the state's coat of arms in the center. The coat of arms has a sailor and a miner on each side of a shield. The shield has symbols for farming, mining, sailing, and manufacturing. Above the shield is a badger. Wisconsin's nickname is the Badger State. In 1979 officials added the state's name and the year 1848 to the flag. Wisconsin became a state in 1848.

MINING PRODUCTS

sand and gravel, limestone, lime

MANUFACTURED GOODS

machinery, food products, fabricated metal products, paper, chemicals, electrical equipment, computer and electronic equipment, plastics and rubber products

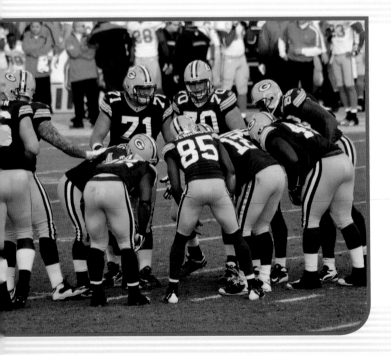

FARM PRODUCTS

cheese, milk, butter, corn, snap beans, cranberries, cherries, beef cattle, hay

PROFESSIONAL SPORTS TEAMS

Milwaukee Brewers (MLB)
Milwaukee Bucks (NBA)
Green Bay Packers (NFL)

WISCONSIN TIMELINE

1620
The Pilgrims establish a colony in the New World in present-day Massachusetts.

1634
French explorer Jean Nicolet canoes across Lake Michigan from Canada. He arrives on the shores of Green Bay and meets American Indians.

1673
French explorers Jacques Marquette and Louis Jolliet travel through Wisconsin.

1763
The British defeat the French in the French and Indian War (1754–1763). The British gain control of all the land east of the Mississippi River, including Wisconsin.

1783
The American colonies win independence from Great Britain in the Revolutionary War (1775–1783). Wisconsin becomes part of the United States.

1832
The U.S. Army defeats American Indians in the Black Hawk War in Wisconsin and Illinois. The American Indians had fought to get their land back.

1836
U.S. Congress creates the Wisconsin Territory.

1848
Wisconsin becomes the 30th state on May 29.

1854
Leaders who are against slavery meet in Ripon in eastern Wisconsin. They want to stop slavery from spreading throughout U.S. territories. The Republican Party begins to form at this meeting.

1856 — Margaretha Meyer Schurz opens the nation's first kindergarten in her home in Watertown in eastern Wisconsin.

1861–1865 — The Union and the Confederacy fight the Civil War. Wisconsin fights for the Union, providing more than 90,000 soldiers. They fight in every major battle of the Civil War. More than 12,000 of them die.

1871 — The Peshtigo forest fire burns in northeastern Wisconsin on October 8. The fire causes more than 1,200 deaths and destroys more than $5 million worth of property. It is one of the worst disasters in Wisconsin history.

1900 Robert M. La Follette Sr. is elected governor of Wisconsin. He carries out many new reforms in the state, including protecting workers' rights.

1914–1918 World War I is fought; the United States enters the war in 1917.

1939–1945 World War II is fought; the United States enters the war in 1941.

1976 Attorney and professor Shirley Abrahamson becomes the first woman on the Wisconsin Supreme Court.

1987 Wisconsin establishes a lottery to raise money for the state.

2001 U.S. President George W. Bush appoints Wisconsin governor Tommy Thompson to be the Health and Human Services secretary.

2012 Paul Ryan, a U.S. Congressman from Wisconsin, is named the Republican Party nominee for vice president in the 2012 presidential election. He runs with Republican presidential nominee Mitt Romney. They lose the election to Barack Obama and Joe Biden. Ryan is re-elected to Congress.

2015 Congressman Paul Ryan is elected as Speaker for the House of Representatives.

Glossary

census *(SEN-suhss)*—an official count of all the people living in a country or district

diverse *(dye-VURSS)*—varied or assorted

economy *(i-KON-uh-mee)*—the ways in which a country handles its money and resources

executive *(ig-ZE-kyuh-tiv)*—the branch of government that makes sure laws are followed

immigrant *(IM-uh-gruhnt)*—someone who comes from one country to live permanently in another country

industry *(IN-duh-stree)*—a business which produces a product or provides a service

judicial *(joo-DISH-uhl)*—to do with the branch of government that explains and interprets the laws

legislature *(LEJ-iss-lay-chur)*—a group of elected officials who have the power to make or change laws for a country or state

peninsula *(puh-NIN-suh-luh)*—a piece of land that sticks out from a larger land mass and is almost completely surrounded by water

tourism *(TOOR-i-zuhm)*—the business of taking care of visitors to a country or place

wetland *(WET-luhnd)*—an area of land covered by water and plants; marshes, swamps, and bogs are wetlands

Read More

Dornfeld, Margaret. *Wisconsin: The Badger State.* It's My State! New York: Cavendish Square Publishing, 2015.

Ganeri, Anita. *United States of America: A Benjamin Blog and His Inquisitive Dog Guide.* Country Guides. Chicago: Heinemann Raintree, 2015.

Wittekind, Erika. *What's Great About Wisconsin?* Our Great States. Minneapolis: Lerner Publications, 2015.

Internet Sites

FactHound offers a safe, fun way to find Internet sites related to this book. All of the sites on FactHound have been researched by our staff.

Here's all you do:

Visit *www.facthound.com*

Type in this code: 9781515704386

 Check out projects, games and lots more at
www.capstonekids.com

Critical Thinking Using the Common Core

1. Wisconsin is shaped like a big mitten. The "thumb" is the Door Peninsula. What is a peninsula? (Craft and Structure)

2. What activities do visitors enjoy at Wisconsin Dells? (Key Ideas and Details)

3. Take a look at the graph on page 16. What percentage of Wisconsin's population is Hispanic/Latino? (Craft and Structure)

Index